WRITTEN BY PAMELA ROSE

ILLUSTRATED BY ANTHONY VALBIRO

EDITING ADVISOR KATHY ZACCAGNINO

2016 Revised reprint; 2009 first print
ISBN# 9781607433118

THIS BOOK IS DEDICATED TO

AMANDA AND ROBBIE

MY TWO WONDERFUL KIDS

WHO MAKE ME TIRED BUT KEEP

ME HAPPY

AND TO MY MOM AND ALL MOMS

WHO NEED A

"TIME OUT"

DID YOU KNOW THAT MOMS

HAVE TEN ARMS?

OCTAMOM
HOME WORK

AND WHEN SHE GETS ON
THE PHONE SHE BECOMES A
HUMAN MAGNET.

WHO'S THAT HONEY?
I NEED MY BRUSH DESPERATELY!
MA! MA! MA! MA! MA!

OF COURSE THE BATHROOM IS MOM'S OFFICIAL PLACE OF BUSINESS.

NO APPOINTMENT NECESSARY!

OUT TO LUNCH
WHICH ONE, HON?
MA MA MA MA MA.
HELP!

WATCHING TV HAS BECOME MORE THAN A FAVORITE PASTIME, ITS BECOME AN OLYMPIC EVENT.

LET THE GAMES BEGIN!

AND ONCE MOM CLEANS A SPACE, THE FAMILY HAS FOUND THEIR NEW FAVORITE SPOT.

MOM'S TAXI SERVICE IS ALWAYS AVAILABLE
GIRL SCOUT COOKIES

YEAR ROUND ... TWENTY-FOUR SEVEN

AND WHEN MOMS DAY IS
FINALLY DONE THERE IS NO
ROOM FOR MOMMY.

WELL NOT ANYMORE!

MOM NEEDS A
TIME OUT!

A TIME OUT...ON THE PHONE.

A TIME OUT...TO RELAX IN THE BATH.

A TIME OUT...TO WATCH HER FAVORITE SHOW ON TV.

A TIME OUT...TO FEEL THE SUN ON HER FACE AND THE BREEZE IN HER HAIR ON THE SWING.

A TIME OUT...TO SING ON
THE TOP OF HER LUNGS IN
THE CAR LIKE A ROCK STAR.

AND A TIME OUT...TO DREAM

AT BEDTIME.

BUT ALWAYS
REMEMBER...MOM NEVER
NEEDS A TIME OUT FROM
YOUR LOVE.

HAPPY·WE·LOVE·YOU·DAY

MOM'S WISH LIST:

1.

2.

3.

Pamela Rose is a Jill of all trades; art teacher, radio show host, artist, singer, dancer, li-brarian, caregiver and full time mom. She knows the feeling of being pulled in all directions. As a busy woman of the 21st century, she thought moms like her needed a laugh as well as a "Time Out." Hence, this book... which she hopes you will enjoy.

BELIEVE!